ASK ME WHAT MY MOTHER DOES

KATHERINE LEINER

Photographs by MICHAEL H. ARTHUR

ASK ME WHAT MY MOTHER DOES

Franklin Watts | New York | London | 1978

To my parents, who helped me understand.
To Dylan, so that he may.

ACKNOWLEDGMENTS

Many thanks to all of the women who so willingly allowed us to photograph them in their work:
V. Baker; Carolyn Billie; Denise Braasch; Norma B. Bradshaw; Lisa Chess; Marylee Gowland;
Rhonda E. Hall; Rose Hammel; Josephine B. Isabel-Jones, M.D.; Jane Kagon; Lee Kay; Joanne
Dempsey Klein; Maryann LaVasser; Molly McGettigan; Sang-enn Noh; Maryann Quinn; Fredricka B. Samuels.

Although not all the women who appear in this book are mothers, they represent the kinds of
professions available to all women, including mothers.

Additional photographs by: *Los Angeles Times,* Michael Mally—Steeplejill; A. P. Schwab—carpenter at sawhorse, musician, lawyer at desk, pediatrician with child and stethoscope; Leonard
Stein—Katherine and Dylan Leiner.

Cover and book design and graphics by
Nicholas Krenitsky

Library of Congress Cataloging in Publication Data

Leiner, Katherine.
  Ask me what my mother does.

  SUMMARY: Text and illustrations describe the
jobs of seventeen working mothers.
  1. Mothers—Employment—United States—Juvenile literature. [1. Mothers—Employment] I. Title.
HD6055.L4   331.4   77-17375
ISBN 0-531-00118-0

CONTENTS

Mothers are busy people. They work at taking care of their children and their houses. Many also have jobs away from home. Right now there are more than 35 million working mothers in America. This book shows some of the many jobs they do.

If your mother works, find out what she does. Ask what other mothers do. What do you think you would like to do when you are an adult? The mothers in this book might give you some ideas.

This mother is a woman in high places. She is a **STEEPLEJILL**. She paints water tanks, radio towers, church steeples, smokestacks, and flagpoles. It is her job to see that these things are painted before they begin to rust. Once the rust begins, there is almost no way to stop it. Rust will cause the metal to rot away.

Sometimes a steeplejill is called on to remove a bird's nest from a church steeple. She must do this carefully so as not to harm the birds. It's a dangerous job that most people are afraid to do, so the pay is high.

A steeplejill knows how to climb. Her arms are strong. She uses a special belt to make her job safer. This belt is called a safety harness. On it she hangs her paintbrush and other tools.

She ties the safety harness to the pole with a knot that won't slip. It's called a square knot. Here is how she ties it. Left over right, right over left. Try tying a square knot yourself. Square knots are also good for tying packages. Most people use a kind of square knot to tie their shoes.

This mother is a **CARPENTER**. She has been building houses for five years. Before she was able to build them herself, she worked with people who taught her. For six years she learned the "tricks of the trade" from carpenters who knew more than she did.

These are some of the tools that she has learned how to work with: Handsaw, metal saw, electric saw, jigsaw, hacksaw, drill, screwdriver, file, pliers, hammer, tack hammer, monkey wrench, pickax, tape measure, folding ruler, sawhorse, sander, and level.

A screwdriver is used to turn and tighten screws.

A drill is used to make holes for screws and nails in wood, plaster, concrete, or metal.

A file is made of steel with a rough surface. It is used for smoothing wood, metal, plastic, and sometimes glass.

A tape measure is used for measuring length, height, and depth.

A sander is a machine that is used to level, smooth, or remove wood.

A sawhorse is a rack on which wood is placed for sawing.

A level is used to measure if the surface of something is even.

A carpenter wears an apron to hold all her tools close at hand.

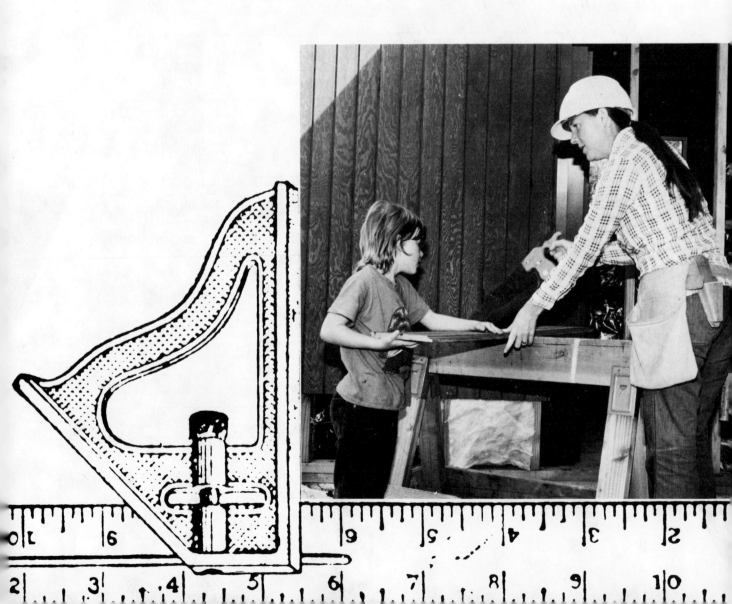

file

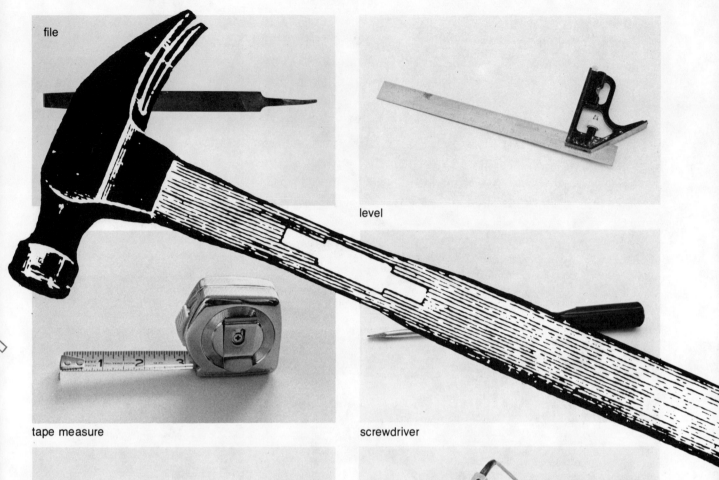

level

tape measure

screwdriver

hand drill

sander

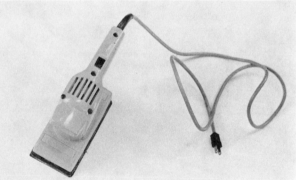

electric drill

carpenter's apron

A carpenter usually starts to build a house by laying the foundation. The foundation is made of concrete. It keeps the house from sinking into the ground.

Next she builds the frame. This frame is made of wood. The inside and outside will be nailed to the frame.

In between the frame and walls there will be a stuffing called insulation. Insulation helps keep the house warm in the winter and cool in the summer.

Next the carpenter puts on the roof. First waterproof paper is laid. That is then covered with thin pieces of wood or asbestos called shingles.

Later the floor is laid. Then she will put in the windows, doors, and locks. Finally she will hand the keys to the new owner!

A photograph is a picture made with a camera. Photo comes from a Greek word meaning light. Graph comes from a Greek word meaning written. A camera picture is an image made with rays of light.

This mother is a **PHOTOGRAPHER**. In her work she takes photographs for newspapers, magazines, and books. Her job is to tell a story through pictures. She spends many hours a day looking for interesting people and places to photograph.

She also spends many hours developing the film and making prints. She does this in her darkroom. While she is making prints from the negatives, a photographer can do tricky things like:

MULTIPLE IMAGES—putting one or more pictures on the same piece of paper.

PHOTOGRAMS—placing an object on the special photographic paper and turning the light on.

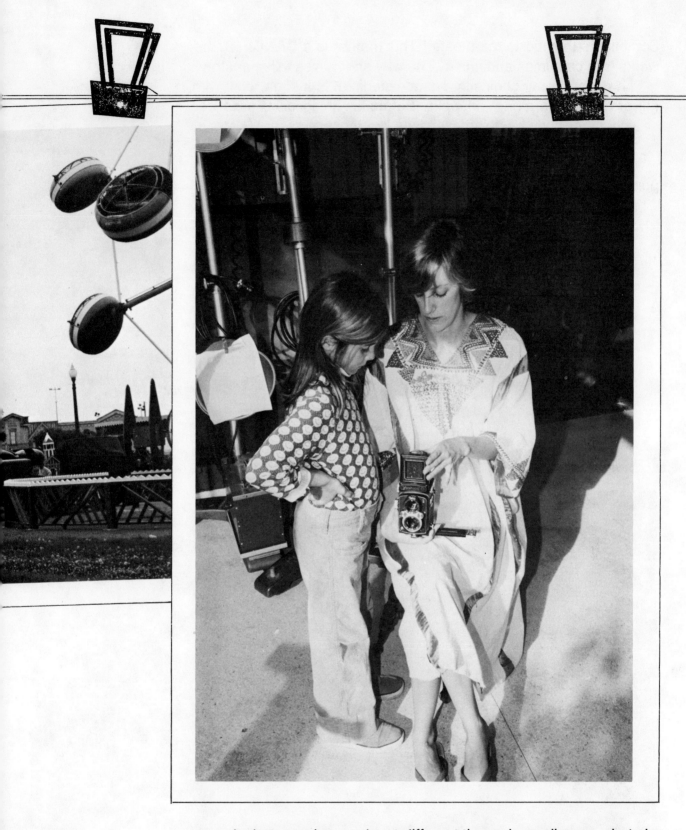

A photographer works at different times depending on what she has to photograph. Sometimes she has to work on weekends. This mother usually takes her children with her.

Sometimes they go to the theater! This mother is a **DANCER**. She works with costumes and music. The way she moves tells her story.

A dancer's day begins in a dance studio. It is a large room with mirrors and bars along the walls. Before anything else, a dancer stretches her body by doing exercises like these:

Releve—on tiptoes.

Arabesque—to the side with one leg raised and the other on its point.

Splits!

After that, she practices the five ballet positions again and again.

This mother makes music. She is a **MUSICIAN**. She has been playing the cello since she was nine years old. Now she plays with a large orchestra. She also practices at home.

Here is one of her favorite songs: *Knowing That You're My Friend*.

Many children walk to school. This mother is a **CROSSING GUARD**. She tells children when it is safe to walk. She also teaches children about crossing streets. Here are her rules:

1. Always cross at a light or crosswalk.
2. Look both ways before crossing.
3. Listen for a car you might not see.
4. Walk, don't run!

Some children take the bus to school. So does this mother! She's a
BUS DRIVER. Her job is to drive children to school. She uses the
lights, turn signals, horn, brakes, and rear-view mirrors to see that
the ride is a safe one. Children use their seatbelts!

This mother is a **POLICE OFFICER**. She protects people and property. Sometimes she'll spot trouble from the air and can call for an ambulance or other police officers to help. She knows how to quiet crowds and direct traffic. She also knows how to handle weapons.

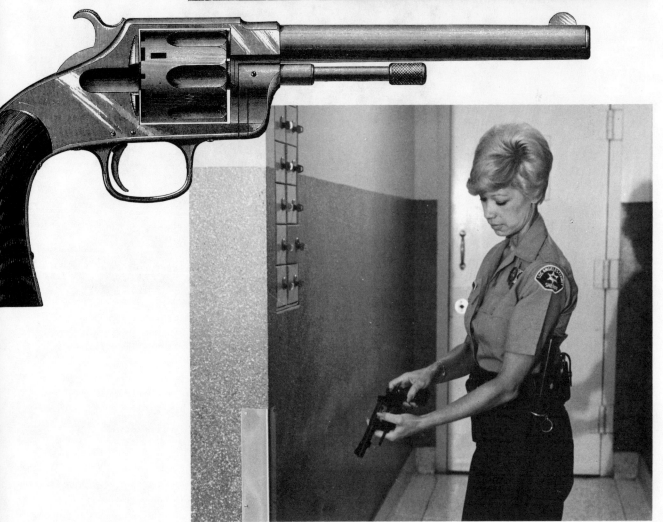

Sometimes she works at the police station, receiving reports of trouble and sending out help. More than three-quarters of her work is done in the police station. The rest of her work is done riding around in her squad car keeping order. She makes about five arrests a week.

There are over one million laws in the United States. This mother helps to see that they are obeyed.

A **LAWYER**'s job is to know and understand the law. There are many different kinds of laws. There are also many different kinds of lawyers. Some are tax lawyers, military lawyers, family lawyers, property lawyers, and criminal lawyers.

This mother is a personal injury lawyer. She handles cases that have to do with accidents between two or more people. She looks into the facts of a case and studies the laws that deal with that kind of case. She speaks for her client in court.

The court is run by a **JUDGE**. This mother is a judge. She also understands the law. In every case she listens to two lawyers who present the two sides of a problem. One side, the plaintiff, is complaining about the other side, the defendant. In some cases the police officer may go to court as a witness. Then she tells what she knows about the case.

After the judge has heard both sides, she sometimes decides who will win the case—the plaintiff or the defendant. Other times she tells a jury to decide.

A jury is a group of people, usually twelve. They listen to both sides of the story. They also listen to the judge tell them about the laws. They go out of the courtroom and talk about the facts until they have made a decision.

This mother types 110 words a minute,
answers the telephone, opens all the
mail, and sets up important appointments.
She is a <u>Secretary</u>.

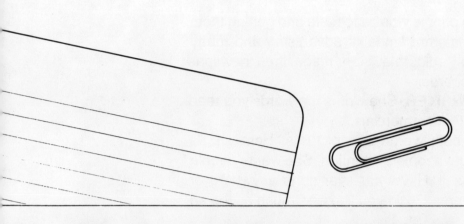

This mother spends most of her working hours at a desk. She types 110 words a minute, answers the telephone, opens all the mail, and sets up important appointments. She is a **SECRETARY**.

Secretaries know how to use a lot of different machines. Many of them can also write in a kind of code called shorthand.

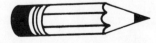

Advertising is a way of telling people what is for sale and getting them to buy it. There are many different kinds of advertising and many different places to advertise: Radio, television, magazines, newspapers, posters, mail, and billboards.

This mother is a **COPYWRITER**. She writes the words you read in ads or hear in radio and TV commercials.

A copywriter thinks in both words and pictures. Here she is putting words to pictures to get people's attention. She wants people to like what she's trying to sell. Have you ever gone anywhere or bought anything because of an ad? Did you like it as much as the ad said you would?

...ays, "Everything fresh, everyday!" This mother runs her ...ss. She is a **BAKER**.

...akes all kinds of things like doughnuts, sweet rolls, and ...e also bakes many different kinds of bread in her store: whole wheat, rye, corn, molasses, nut, pumpkin, and squash. Her best-selling bread is whole wheat.

In one week, she uses 840 pounds (378 kg) of flour, 36 gallons (165 l) of milk, 36 ounces (1020 g) of baking soda, and 22.5 pounds (10.2 kg) of yeast in her breads. Other best-sellers in the store are birthday cakes. She sells at least 40 cakes a week.

Her children like everything she bakes. Their favorite is MOM'S MARSHMALLOWS! Have you ever had homemade marshmallows?
You will need:

electric mixer
mixing bowl
cup
heavy pan
cooking thermometer
8″ by 12″ (20 by 30 cm) pan
timer
scissors
3 tablespoons (45 ml) gelatin
½ cup (120 ml) cold water
2 cups (480 ml) sugar
¾ cup (180 ml) light corn syrup
½ cup (120 ml) water
¼ teaspoon (1 ml) salt
2 tablespoons (30 ml) vanilla extract
cornstarch

1. Sprinkle the gelatin into ½ cup of cold water in the mixing bowl and let it stand for 1 hour.

2. Then in about ½ hour start to prepare a syrup by placing the heavy pan over low heat and stirring in the 2 cups sugar, ¾ cup of corn syrup, ½ cup water, and ¼ teaspoon salt until everything is dissolved.

3. When the mixture starts to boil (bubbles will appear), turn your timer on for 3 minutes, put your thermometer in the mixture, and cover the pan. Let the mixture cook until the thermometer reaches 240 degrees F (115° C)—no longer, or you'll make the marshmallows too hard.

4. Now, remove the pan from the heat and pour the mixture slowly over the gelatin, at the same time beating the mixture with the electric mixer. After all the mixture has been poured, beat the mixture for about 15 minutes. Use your timer.

5. When the mixture is good and thick and still warm, add the 2 teaspoons of vanilla extract.

6. Dust a little cornstarch into the 8″ by 12″ pan. Pour or spoon the mixture into the pan. Let it dry for 12 hours.

7. When you get up the next day, cut it into squares either with scissors or a knife. Either of these utensils should be dusted with cornstarch. This will keep the marshmallows from sticking.

Now try one! All the money in the world couldn't buy a better marshmallow. They will keep until your next barbecue if you put them in a closed tin. Yummm . . . roasted marshmallows.

If you want to save money to buy something, this mother will put it in the bank vault until you need it. She's a **BANK TELLER**. She will give you your own bankbook so you know how much money you have saved. When you want to get your money back, she will get it for you. She also cashes your parents' checks.

A **PEDIATRICIAN** is a doctor who takes care of children. This mom is a pediatrician. She takes care of both healthy and sick children. Healthy children often come to her for shots that keep them from getting measles, mumps, and other diseases. Sick children may have colds or broken bones. Some need operations.

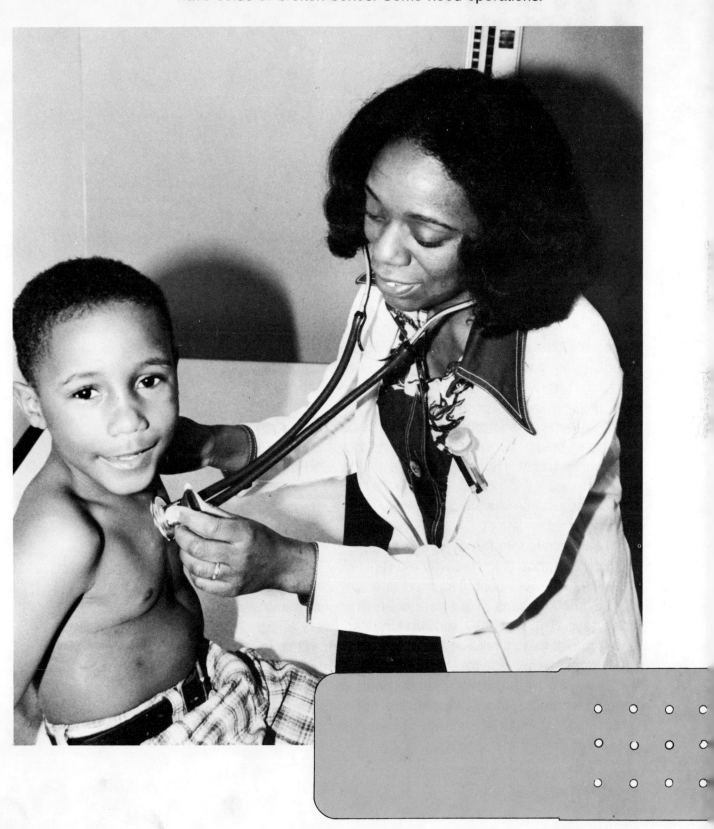

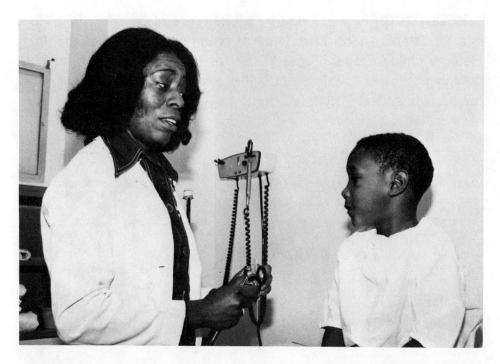

She spends many hours a week in schools teaching children about their bodies.

A pediatrician uses tools to see, feel, and hear what a child's body is doing. This is how she finds clues, called symptoms. Symptoms help her find out why the child is sick. One symptom is fever. Fever is when the body heats up because it is fighting the germs that are making it sick. A thermometer shows how high the fever is.

A sore throat is another symptom. By using a tongue depressor, the doctor holds down the tongue and looks for redness or white spots on the throat. These spots are a clue to what kind of sore throat the child has.

A stethoscope lets the doctor hear what is going on in the lungs. It is also used to listen to a child's heartbeat. The otoscope is a little light used to see into the eyes and ears.

Once the doctor knows why a child is sick, she can decide what medicines will work best. The medicine may come in a pill or liquid form. Sometimes it is given as a shot. Shots don't hurt very much these days. The needles used are small and very sharp.

A pediatrician works at her office and in hospitals. When she goes home at night, she takes her black bag. That's where she keeps her tools. She never knows when her help will be needed, so she is always prepared. Her car has a special license plate. M.D. stands for medical doctor. In an emergency she can park anywhere she needs to and not get a parking ticket.

otoscope

stethoscope

injection needle

thermometer

tongue depressor

All kinds of people have all kinds of problems. This mother is a **SOCIAL WORKER**. She helps people with problems. She works in an adoption agency, finding good homes for children who don't have parents.

A social worker will sometimes place a child with temporary parents. These parents are called foster parents. They act as parents for only a short time while the social worker looks for exactly the right people to be the child's parents.

She needs to know where the child will live, and if the parents will take good care of the child. Once the social worker gets to know the parents and the child, she decides if they will make a happy family.

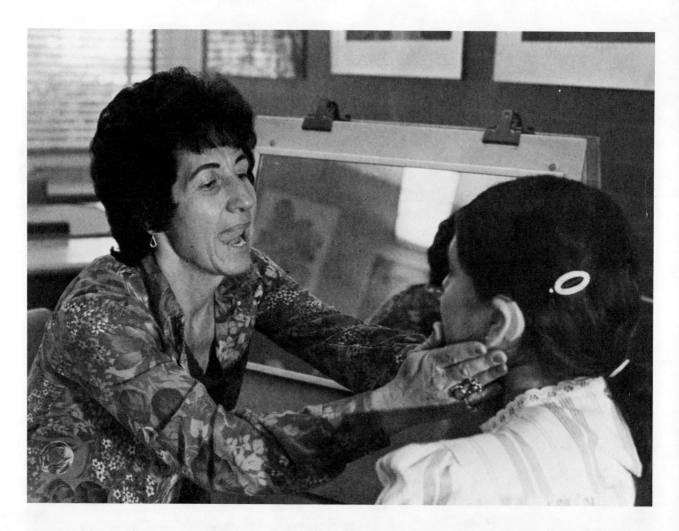

There are many deaf children in the world. Some of them can hear some sounds with the help of a machine called a hearing aid. Sounds go into the machine through a microphone and are made much louder. Then they go along wires to earpieces that children wear in their ears. Some children can't hear at all.

This mother is a **SPECIAL EDUCATION TEACHER**. She works with children who are deaf. She teaches them how to see what another person is saying by the way the person moves her lips. This is called *lip reading*.

Most children learn to talk by repeating the sounds they hear. Children who can't hear learn to speak by feeling words. Put your hand on another person's throat. Do you feel the way the throat moves when the person speaks? This is called the *vibration*. A deaf child feels the vibration in the teacher's throat and watches the teacher's mouth. Then she tries to move her mouth the same way the teacher does. She tries to make the same vibration the teacher has made.

This mother also teaches the deaf children to talk with their hands. This is called *sign language*. There is a sign for every letter and word in our language.

This child is deaf. Her mother taught her how to see words, feel words, and to talk with her hands. Here she is saying, "Ask me what my mother does!" You can say it too!

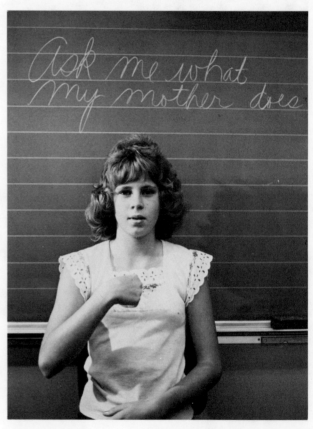

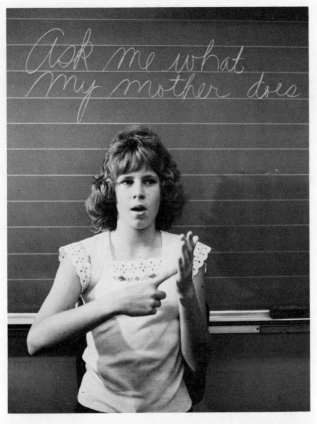

ABOUT THE AUTHOR

KATHERINE LEINER is a mother and a writer too! She lives in Pacific Palisades, California.

ABOUT THE PHOTOGRAPHER

MICHAEL H. ARTHUR is assistant director at the San Diego Center of Photographic Arts. He is a faculty member of South Western College. He lives in La Jolla with his wife.